david BECKHAM

annual

CONTENTS

ZINC 7

© 2003 Zincseven Limited

Written by Robert Louis
Designed by Craig Randall

Published by Zincseven Limted
City Forum
250 City Road
London EC1 2QO

Printed in the E.U.

GOLDEN BOY

The opening chapter in David Beckham's Real life story was written 28 years ago...

The child destined to become the Golden Boy of English soccer entered the world on 2nd May 1975, under the starsign Taurus.

Astrologically speaking, being a Taurean marks him as determined, sensitive, loyal and steady. It places him among the most reliable of people, with an occasional tendency to do something absolutely explosive – a handy trait for a soccer star!

Christened David Robert Joseph, he was the middle child (between two sisters) born to Ted and Sandra Beckham, in Leytonstone, East London. He grew into a happy-go-lucky boy whose favourite pastime from a very early age was, you've guessed it...football.

He enjoyed practically every other sport too, once winning a 1500 metres race by a whole lap – and he was pretty adept at rugby, basketball and swimming. But it was football that won out every time.

David naturally became an automatic choice as a striker for his school teams. He was a prolific goal-getter, too, notching over 100 strikes in three seasons for boys' team Ridgeway Rovers.

It soon became obvious that the lively young Beckham had the potential to develop into a better than average player and, by all accounts, he was very determined to do exactly that. In fact, as a schoolboy he decided that he would one day earn his living as a professional footballer. And whenever he wasn't playing in a match he would practise constantly, honing his talent and polishing those natural-born skills of his.

All that ambition, training and dedication would eventually pay off – in the best and the biggest way possible...

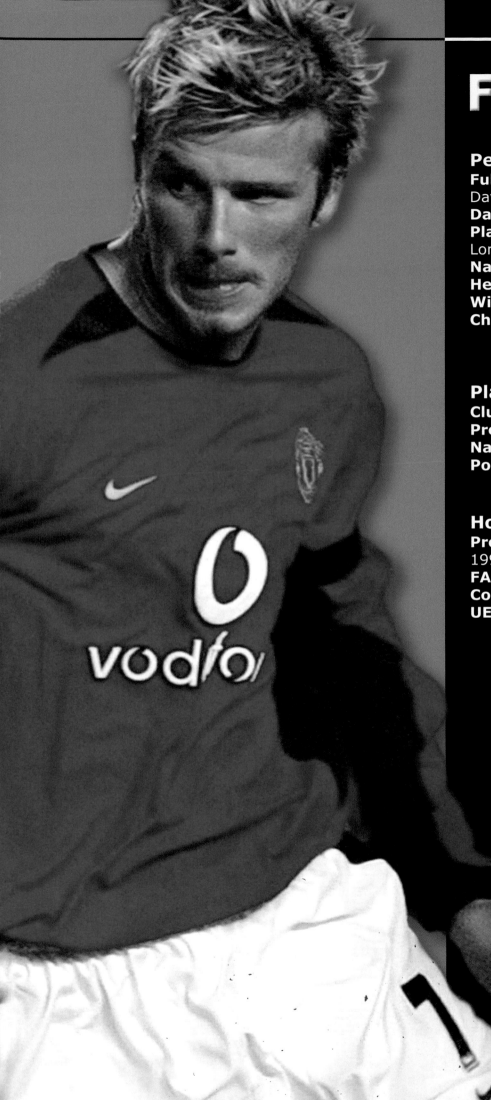

FAST FACTS

Personal Info
Full Name:
David Robert Joseph Beckham
Date of Birth: 2 May 1975
Place of Birth: Leytonstone, London
Nationality: English
Height: 5ft 11in
Wife: Victoria
Children: Brooklyn and Romeo

Player Profile
Club: Real Madrid
Previous Club: Manchester United
National Team: England
Position: Midfield

Honours Won
Premier League: 1996, 1997, 1999, 2000, 2001, 2003
FA Cup: 1996, 1999
Community Shield: 1996, 1997
UEFA Champions League: 1999

SHOWI
PROMI

Beckham's road to Real Madrid started at Ridgeway Rovers boys' team.

Guess what? David might easily have become a Spurs, Arsenal or West Ham star!

Born and raised in Leytonstone, a Greater London town bordering the East End, it would have been perfectly natural if the young Becks had followed one of the capital city's big soccer clubs (his grandad was a Tottenham fan, after all).

But David was committed to Manchester United right from the start, a passion encouraged by his father who was also a lifelong United devotee. And so the Old Trafford club became the focus for the boy's big ambitions. Trouble was, Leytonstone lay over 200 miles away from Manchester and David often wondered just how United could possible notice him!

In fact, it was Tottenham who first recognised his potential, inviting him along for training with other promising young players. David accepted the offer – and reportedly sported his favourite 'Man U' replica shirt during Spurs' coaching sessions.

David's big hero in the 1980s was legendary Bryan Robson, the player who wore Manchester United's No. 7 shirt week-in and week-out. Imagine what a thrilling day it must have been for the youngster, when chosen as United's mascot for a match against the Hammers at Upton Park. He must have been bubbling over with pride while running onto the pitch alongside the great 'Robbo'.

In 1986, David reached the finals of a nationwide Soccer Skills competition run by Bobby Charlton's world renowned Soccer School. According to Sir Bobby, the boy Beckham really stood out and easily won his age group with a record points tally. His prize was a two weeks stay with Spanish giants and European super-club Barcelona. Then coached by Terry Venables, Barca boasted British strikers Gary Lineker, Steve Archibald and Mark Hughes among their ranks and meeting these superstars strengthened Becks' ambitions.

It was soon after his return from Spain, and no doubt at the advice of the great Bobby

Young David with his first team, Ridgeway Rovers

Charlton, that Manchester United came calling with the offer of a series of trials. When his mum told him the news, David apparently burst into tears of relief.

Under Alex Ferguson's expert guidance, United had become *the* leading club for youth development and there were already many talented youngsters in the Old Trafford fold. They included Ryan Giggs, Nicky Butt, Paul Scholes and the Neville brothers Gary and Phil. The club's coaches monitored David's progress closely before deciding, in July 1991, that he was ready to join those future stars as an Old Trafford trainee.

Leaving his family proved quite a wrench. But United are the best in the business when it comes to looking after their

When Torpedo Moscow visited Old Trafford for a UEFA Cup tie that September, he was listed as a substitute but didn't play. In the following week's League Cup tie at Brighton David made a first-team appearance at last, coming on as a 70th-minute sub for Andrei Kanchelskis in a 1-1 draw. Four months later he was delighted to accept Manchester United's offer of professional terms.

United topped the new Premier League that season – their first top flight title success since 1966-67, and the catalyst for a long-awaited return to Europe's biggest competition, the UEFA Champions' League. A year later United achieved the 1993-94 League and FA Cup 'double'. Old Trafford was definitely *the* place to be.

United achieved the 1993-94 League and FA Cup 'double'. Old Trafford was definitely the place to be.

young charges and he soon felt at ease – especially when living at club-approved lodgings close to United's famous training ground, The Cliff. It was an exciting time to be there – the place was buzzing with expectation as Fergie shrewdly gathered together the core of his future squad.

In the spring of 1992 David played in United's FA Youth Cup semi-final 2nd leg success against Spurs. Then he scored the second goal in a 3-1 victory against Crystal Palace at Selhurst Park in the first-leg of the final. He was also in the line-up when United finished the job on 15 May 1992, only a few days after his 17th birthday. With regular first-teamer Ryan Giggs in the side, they beat Palace 3-2 at Old Trafford in the 2nd leg for a 6-3 aggregate win. It was the club's first FA Youth Cup success since 1964 – and David Beckham collected his first major medal.

Alex Ferguson selected David as a non-playing sub against Swedish champions Gothenburg in a Champions' League fixture on 14 September 1994 – and he made his first first team start a week later, at Port Vale in the League Cup 2nd Round. His home debut came in the return game when Vale visited Old Trafford on 5 October. He played in midfield and provided the corner-kick from which David May scored United's second goal in a 2-0 victory.

Next came some important appearances against Newcastle at a packed St James' Park and against Turkish side Galatasaray in the European Champions' League. United were already out of the running for Euro honours, so Alex Ferguson decided to give David the biggest game of his career to date – a faith repaid when he netted United's second goal in a 4-2 win.

With United comfortably ahead against Wrexham in the FA

Cup 4th Round on 28 January 1995, David was sent on as a 75th-minute sub. Now he had appeared in every competition except the League – but when *that* debut came it wasn't in United's colours.

In an experience-gathering exercise he was loaned out to Preston who were going well in the 1994-95 Third Division promotion race. Taking to the challenge like the proverbial duck to water, he came off the bench against Doncaster at Deepdale on 4 March '95 and proceeded to score his first ever league goal, in a 2-2 draw. He played in further Preston victories against Fulham (scoring again), Bury and Exeter, and in a draw at Lincoln.

On his return to United he finally made his Premiership debut in a 0-0 draw with Leeds at Old Trafford and was soon in contention for a regular first team place as the Red Devils challenged yet again for the championship. Their sights were also set on Wembley and the FA Cup. Sheffield United, Wrexham, Leeds and QPR were all eliminated as United powered to a semi-final meeting with Crystal Palace at Villa Park. David played a little over half the match which ended all-square at 2-2. Three days later Manchester United won the replay 2-0 to reach their 13th FA Cup final.

However, the season was to end in frustration. A last day defeat at West Ham meant United were pipped in the title race by Blackburn. Then they lost 1-0 to Everton in the FA Cup Final at Wembley. Amid all of this activity David made three more Premiership appearances – at Leicester, where he was involved in the creation of two goals in a 4-0 victory; against Chelsea in a 0-0 draw at Old Trafford and in a 3-2 win at Coventry

Despite United's disappointing finish David Beckham had begun to make himself noticed by the Old Trafford faithful – and in the summer he was selected for England's Under-21 squad for the annual Toulon Tournament in France. Things were looking good.

IF HE'S GOOD ENOUGH...

In the 1995-96 season, Beckham found himself thrown in at the deep end.

In June 1995 David was thrilled when awarded his England Under-21 debut against Brazil in the annual Toulon Tournament in France. England lost 2-0 that day, but in his next appearance against Malaysia they won 2-0. He also played in a 1-0 win against Angola and a 2-0 defeat by France.

Having made the breakthrough into Manchester United's first team towards the end of the previous season, David then encountered a twist of fate in the '95-96 campaign.

Alex Ferguson had intended to keep his latest protégé on the sidelines for a while longer and introduce him gradually to the tougher side of top flight football, but an injury to Ryan Giggs and the departure of Andrei Kanchelskis to Everton, meant that Becks was given an unexpected and extended run early in the season.

Proudly wearing his No. 24 squad number in a youthful line-up, he scored United's opening goal of the campaign in a 3-1 defeat by Aston Villa. It was a pretty shaky start that caused TV pundit Alan Hansen to remark 'You can't win anything with kids!' Fergie and his squad were soon to disprove the Scotsman's theory with what became a phenomenally successful season for the club.

Later, when Giggsy returned to the team, David retained *his* first-team place, playing up-front alongside quicksilver striker Andy Cole. This prominent forward role helped the youngster to take his season's tally to seven goals in 33 League appearances as United won a breathtaking neck-and-neck race with Newcastle to lift their third Premier League title. Among Beckham's contributions to this great success were goals against Blackburn, Coventry, Chelsea and Bolton, plus two in a 5-0 win against Nottingham Forest. He also played his part

thirteen

1.

'You can't win anything with kids!' – Alan Hansen (oops!)

when they wrapped up the title with a 3-1 victory at Middlesbrough on the last day.

In that season's FA Cup campaign, David had played in the 2-2 draw with Sunderland in the Third Round at Old Trafford, but he was suspended for the replay at Roker Park which United won 2-0. They next eliminated Reading with a 3-0 scoreline in the Fourth Round, without David's help. In the Fifth Round they disposed of neighbours Manchester City, again without his involvement. He didn't play in the Sixth Round defeat of Southampton either, when the Old Trafford crowd saw United march into the semi-finals with a 2-0 win.

But he was in the semi-final line-up against Chelsea at Villa Park – and netted his most vital goal of the season in the match. Ruud Gullit had scored for the Blues, Andy Cole had scored for the Reds, but it was David's 58th-minute strike that earned United a 2-1 victory and took them to a Wembley showdown with Liverpool.

By the time David lined-up in the 1996 FA Cup final on 11 May, United had already been crowned Premiership champions. Now, in order to become the first club to achieve the League and FA Cup 'double' twice, they had to beat Liverpool beneath Wembley's twin towers.

It was Eric Cantona – the then-wearer of the 'United 7' shirt so keenly coveted by David Beckham – who won the day with a flash of absolute brilliance. In the 86th minute of an otherwise dreary game, United's French magician pulled the proverbial rabbit out of the hat to score the only goal of the afternoon with a sublime piece of individual skill. David now had a Championship medal and an FA Cup winners' medal to his name after just two seasons of top level football. That's more than the majority of players achieve in a lifetime.

Alex Ferguson's selection of Beckham in United's side had also proved the wisdom of the old football adage so often applied to promising youngsters. 'If he's good enough, he's old enough.' It also helped to make Alan Hansen eat his hasty words!

Although he had spent some time in that forward role, it was generally agreed that the young Beckham was a true midfield playmaker capable of running a game with far seeing intelligence and accurate long passes. This was recognised by England who gave him five more outings in the Under-21 team – against Portugal (twice), Austria (as a sub), Belgium and Angola .

That summer he watched along with the rest of the country as Terry Venables steered England to the Euro '96 quarter-finals . As Alan Shearer, Paul Gascoigne, Teddy Sheringham and company came so close to glory before going out on penalties against Germany, David must have been wondering when his own senior debut would come along. Our boy didn't have long to wait.

2.

3.

MANCHESTER UNITED
SEASON 1995-96

PREMIERSHIP		Position: 1st		
19 Aug	Aston Villa	A	L	1-3
23 Aug	West Ham United	H	W	2-1
26 Aug	Wimbledon	H	W	3-1
28 Aug	Blackburn Rovers	A	W	2-1
09 Sep	Everton	A	W	3-2
16 Sep	Bolton Wanderers	H	W	3-0
23 Sep	Sheffield Wed	A	D	0-0
01 Oct	Liverpool	H	D	2-2
14 Oct	Manchester City	H	W	1-0
21 Oct	Chelsea	A	W	4-1
28 Oct	Middlesbrough	H	W	2-0
04 Nov	Arsenal	A	L	0-1
18 Nov	Southampton	H	W	4-1
22 Nov	Coventry City	A	W	4-0
27 Nov	Nottingham F.	A	D	1-1
02 Dec	Chelsea	H	D	1-1
09 Dec	Sheffield Wed	H	D	2-2
17 Dec	Liverpool	A	L	0-2
24 Dec	Leeds United	A	L	1-3
27 Dec	Newcastle United	H	W	2-0
30 Dec	QPR	H	W	2-1
01 Jan	Tottenham Hotspur	A	L	1-4
13 Jan	Aston Villa	H	D	0-0
22 Jan	West Ham United	A	W	1-0
03 Feb	Wimbledon	A	W	4-2
10 Feb	Blackburn Rovers	H	W	1-0
21 Feb	Everton	H	W	2-0
25 Feb	Bolton Wanderers	A	W	6-0
04 Mar	Newcastle United	A	W	1-0
16 Mar	QPR	A	D	1-1
20 Mar	Arsenal	H	W	1-0
24 Mar	Tottenham Hotspur	H	W	1-0
06 Apr	Manchester City	A	W	3-2
08 Apr	Coventry City	H	W	1-0
13 Apr	Southampton	A	L	1-3
17 Apr	Leeds United	H	W	1-0
28 Apr	Nottingham F.	H	W	5-0
05 May	Middlesbrough	A	W	3-0

FA CUP		Winners		
06 Jan	Sunderland	H	D	2-2
16 Jan	Sunderland	A	W	2-1
27 Jan	Reading	A	W	3-0
18 Feb	Manchester City	H	W	2-1
11 Mar	Southampton	H	W	2-0
31 Mar	Chelsea	H	W	2-1
11 May	Liverpool	N	W	1-0

COCA-COLA CUP				
20 Sep	York City	H	L	0-3
03 Oct	York City	A	W	3-1

DB CHALLENGE

MATCH THE MATCH

Name the teams David is playing for and the teams he is playing against.

Answers: see page 61

TRUE OR FALSE?

1. Beckham moved to Barcelona from Man United in June 2003.

2. Man United sold him for £2m.

3. Becks is a free-kick specialist.

4. He has two sons.

5. Real Madrid's colours are pink and yellow.

6. Beckham once played for Brentford on loan from United.

7. He scored a goal against Argentina in the 1998 World Cup.

8. Becks scored for England against Greece in 2000.

9. Becks was born in Leytonstone.

10. His squad number at Manchester United was 7.

SPOT THE DIFFERENCE
Find five differences between the two pictures.

BECKHAM'S WORDSEARCH

Find the words below in the grid. They may be written horizontally, vertically or diagonally.

ENGLAND
VICTORIA
ROMEO
BROOKLYN
FOOTBALL
OLD TRAFFORD
PREMIERSHIP
CORNER KICK
GOAL
CHAMPIONS
UEFA
WORLD CUP
TEAM
MEDAL
TRAINING
REAL MADRID
FREE KICK

```
D S W C H A M P I O N S Q M
G F R E E K I C K W O N T S
T D A F W W R Y R T J P F R N
D F S C D F Y R T O T P A X
H C G V F Y V R R E A R I H
U V O L I T F O H D A N N E
J C A R H C H M G F D M I S
I W L H N B T E V J H N G U
M Y T G T E X O M G J E S B
E H F V R F R O R B A R J P
D B D N F A Q K X I L S U F
A N A T O W W Y I W A H J P
L U Z U O Q O G Q C E I V F
W J X R T S S R W D K P V R
B I L W B D C S L V D L R N
V U I A A F I A H D B Q E N
X E N G L A N D H J C P K D
A F T D L L V Z F A H U S L
D A F F H M G X U W K N P Y
G O L D T R A F F O R D I V
H R E A L M A D R I D H V E
J C S C B R O O K L Y N S E
```

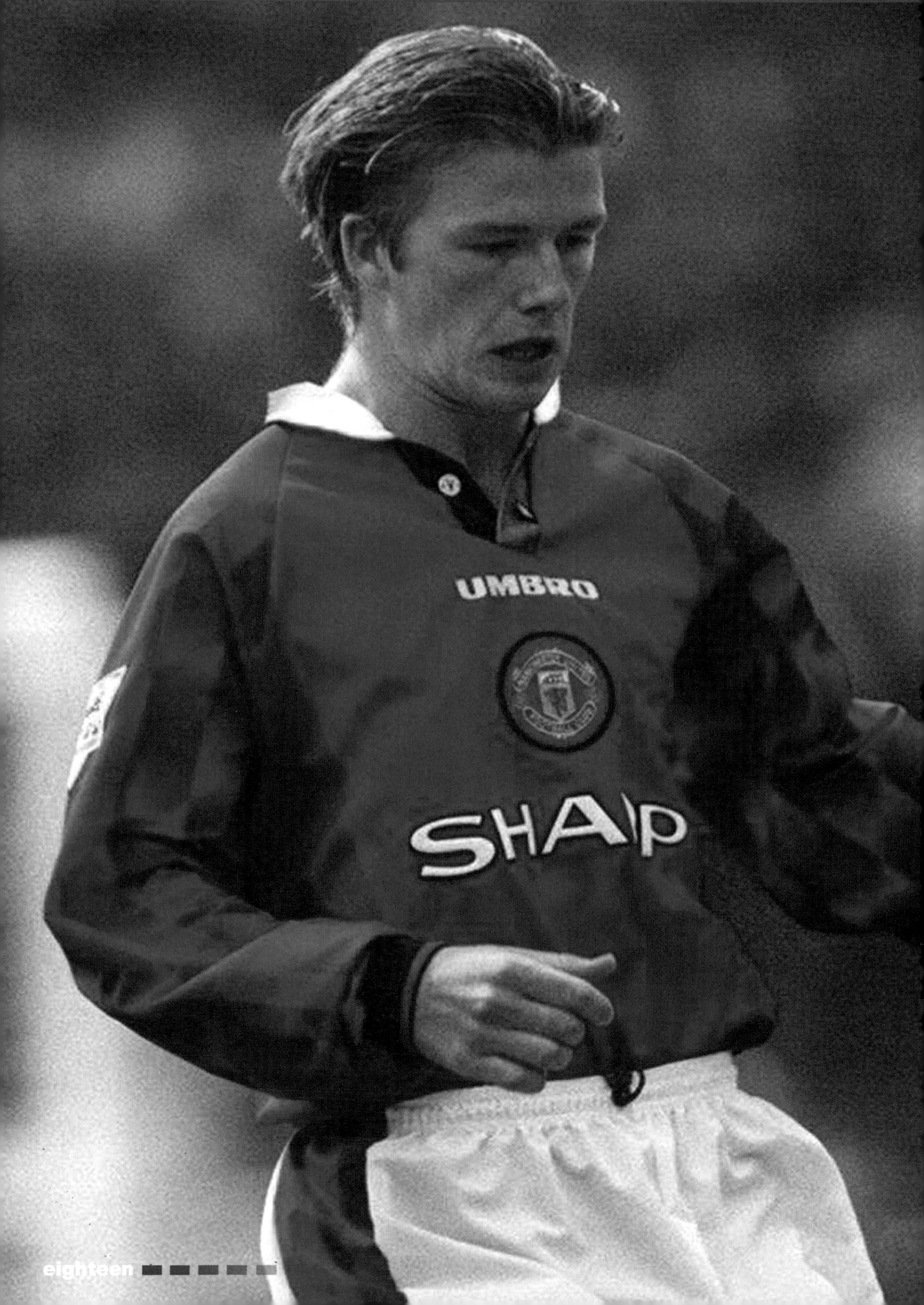
UMBRO
SHARP

WHAT A FANTASTIC GOAL!

David's 1996-97 campaign began with a moment of sheer genius.

The annual FA Charity Shield match at Wembley got David's 1996-97 season off to a great start. He scored a magnificent goal as Manchester United beat Newcastle 3-0. His strike was lobbed from all of 40 yards.

As if that wasn't enough, he then did something similar – only better – in United's opening Premier League game against Wimbledon at Selhurst Park. The Red Devils were 2-0 ahead, through Eric Cantona and Denis Irwin, as the match drew towards its close. It was then that David found himself in possession just inside United's own half some 55 yards from the Dons' goal. From there he noticed that goalkeeper Neil Sullivan had strayed from his line.

Everyone inside Selhurst Park that day will always remember what happened next. Quick as a flash Beckham launched a high ball goalwards. It was already too late for Sullivan by the time he saw it coming. The 'keeper scampered backwards as the ball bounced once before flying into the net behind him for a 3-0 scoreline. Alex Ferguson called it 'the goal of the season' – and there were still 37 more League games left to play!

David was on Cloud Nine and later admitted that he wanted to shake hands with everyone in the stadium. The

United went on to finish top of the table seven points ahead of runners-up Newcastle.

moment was replayed countless times on TV over the coming weeks and made Beckham an instant legend. 'That goal' against Wimbledon would never be forgotten.

The following month saw his elevation into the senior England squad when new England coach Glenn Hoddle selected him for the World Cup qualifier against Moldova on 1 September 1996. David played in right midfield as England enjoyed a great start to their campaign with a 3-0 victory. He would retain his place in the team throughout the qualifying tournament.

As United's season progressed the young star seemed to get better and better as the club challenged for yet more success. There were some more spectacular Beckham goals, most notably against Spurs in the FA Cup Third Round, although United would stumble at the next stage, going out to Wimbledon in a replay. He also netted a great goal against Austrian side Rapid Vienna in the European Champions' League; Man United would reach the semi-final before elimination by Borussia Dortmund.

In the Premiership he netted an all-important equaliser at Derby and the winner against Liverpool at Old Trafford. In late-October he was in the side that experienced an uncharacteristic slump with two major away defeats in succession: 6-3 at Southampton and 5-0 at Newcastle. Then, a 2-1 home defeat by Chelsea completed a list of results that had the cynics saying United's glory days were coming to an end.

But David and his United team-mates pulled themselves out of the slump and would lose only two more games in the remainder of their Premiership programme. He scored in a draw at West Ham and in a 4-0 win against Nottingham Forest on Boxing Day.

Then came a big worry when an ankle injury sustained in January '97 threatened to bring his season to a premature end. But he recovered quickly and got back into full-blooded action, netting an amazing equaliser in the 1-1 draw at Chelsea in February. United went on to finish top of the table seven points ahead of runners-up Newcastle. Becks had played in 36 League games, had netted eight goals and once again had a Championship medal to show for his magnificent efforts. His talents were also recognised by his fellow professionals who voted him 1997's PFA Young Player of the Year.

Meanwhile, David's international career was moving along nicely, with further appearances against Poland and Georgia (twice), and Italy as England kept pace with the Italians at the top of their Qualifying Group for the '98 World Cup finals.

MANCHESTER UNITED SEASON 1996-97

PREMIERSHIP — Position: 1st

Date	Opponent		Result	
17 Aug	Wimbledon	A	W	3-0
21 Aug	Everton	H	D	2-2
25 Aug	Blackburn Rovers	H	D	2-2
04 Sep	Derby County	A	D	
07 Sep	Leeds United	A	W	4-0
14 Sep	Nottingham Forest	H	W	4-1
21 Sep	Aston Villa	A	D	0-0
29 Sep	Tottenham Hotspur	H	W	2-0
12 Oct	Liverpool	H	W	1-0
20 Oct	Newcastle United	A	L	0-5
26 Oct	Southampton	A	L	3-6
02 Nov	Chelsea	H	L	1-2
16 Nov	Arsenal	H	W	1-0
23 Nov	Middlesbrough	A	D	2-2
30 Nov	Leicester City	H	W	3-1
08 Dec	West Ham United	A	D	2-2
18 Dec	Sheffield Wed	A	D	1-1
21 Dec	Sunderland	H	W	5-0
26 Dec	Nottingham F	A	W	4-0
28 Dec	Leeds United	H	W	1-0
01 Jan	Aston Villa	H	D	0-0
12 Jan	Tottenham Hotspur	A	W	2-1
18 Jan	Coventry City	A	W	2-0
29 Jan	Wimbledon	H	W	2-1
01 Feb	Southampton	H	W	2-1
19 Feb	Arsenal	A	W	2-1
22 Feb	Chelsea	A	D	1-1
01 Mar	Coventry City	H	W	3-1
08 Mar	Sunderland	A	L	1-2
15 Mar	Sheffield Wed	H	W	2-0
22 Mar	Everton	A	W	2-0
05 Apr	Derby County	H	L	2-3
12 Apr	Blackburn Rovers	A	W	3-2
19 Apr	Liverpool	A	W	3-1
03 May	Leicester City	A	D	2-2
05 May	Middlesbrough	H	D	3-3
08 May	Newcastle United	H	D	0-0
11 May	West Ham United	H	W	2-0

FA CUP

Date	Opponent		Result	
05 Jan	Tottenham Hotspur	H	W	2-0
25 Jan	Wimbledon	H	D	1-1
04 Feb	Wimbledon	A	L	0-1

COCA-COLA CUP

Date	Opponent		Result	
23 Oct	Swindon Town	H	W	2-0
27 Nov	Leicester City	A	L	0-2

CHAMPIONS LEAGUE

GROUP C - Position 2nd

Date	Opponent			
11 Sep	Juventus	A	L	0-1
25 Sep	Rapid Vienna	H	W	2-0
16 Oct	Fenerbahce	A	W	2-0
30 Oct	Fenerbahce	H	L	0-1
28 Nov	Juventus	H	L	0-1
04 Dec	Rapid Vienna	A	W	2-0

QUARTER-FINAL

05 Mar	FC Porto	H	W	4-0
19 Mar	FC Porto	A	D	0-0

SEMI-FINAL

09 Apr	B Dortmund	A	L	0-1
23 Apr	B Dortmund	H	L	0-1

VICTO & DAV

Early in 1997 Victoria Adams was well on her way to becoming one of the most famous celebrities in the country. As a member of a certain five-piece pop group called the Spice Girls, her face was familiar to everyone – including David Beckham. The young soccer star had even confided to his close friend and team-mate, Gary Neville, that he really fancied the Posh one!

On 22 February 1997, Manchester United travelled to West London to take on Chelsea in the Premiership. On the same day 'Sporty Spice' – Liverpool fan Mel C – decided to introduce Victoria to the wonderful world of football.

The two Girl Power Sisters saw a terrific match, in which David netted a great equaliser to cancel out Chelsea's early lead. Afterwards, the two Spice Girls made their way to the players lounge where she and David somehow managed not to meet one another.

A few weeks later, Sporty and Posh turned up for United's match against Sheffield Wednesday. During the half-time interval the two Spice Girls drew a raffle and were interviewed on local radio. When Victoria was asked who her favourite footballer was, she said that Eric Cantona was pretty cool – and coyly added that 'David Beckham is very good'. Soon after that Victoria and David met and romance blossomed.

It was a story made in newspaper heaven. And, as soon as the love match became known, Victoria and David found themselves dogged by an army of photographers and reporters. They got their revenge when United played Coventry at Old Trafford in August 1997. Victoria was spotted in the crowd wearing a beautiful gold ring on her engagement finger – but it turned out to be a brilliant wind-up by the couple!

Five months later David really proposed to Victoria and she accepted. This time the rings paraded for the cameras were the real thing. The couple were obviously overjoyed and very much in love. Victoria declared herself the happiest girl in the world. 'I'm with the man I know I'm going to grow old and wrinkly with,' she said.

Victoria with the Spice Girls

RED WOES, WORLD

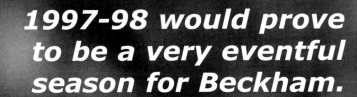

1997-98 would prove to be a very eventful season for Beckham.

CUP BLUES

David scored Man United's winner in the second game of their 1997-98 Premier League campaign. It came against Southampton at Old Trafford soon after he came on as a sub. He scored again against Everton two games later, in a 2-0 victory at Goodison Park. Then a return to Selhurst Park, where he had scored the previous season's wonder goal, produced two super strikes in United's 5-2 defeat of Wimbledon.

That was followed by two stunning Beckham strikes – against Liverpool in a 3-1 Premier League win at Anfield and at Chelsea in the Third Round of the FA Cup, when United won 5-3 to progress in the competition (although they were eventually knocked-out in a Fifth Round replay by Barnsley).

Between late-October and early-April, United were looking good for another title success as they held on to the Premiership

top spot. But it was then that Arsene Wenger's forceful and flamboyant Arsenal caught them up, overtook them and did not let go for the rest of the season. The Gunners also won the 1998 FA Cup final against Newcastle to complete the 'double'. United also lost out in Europe in '97-98, eliminated by Monaco in the Champions' League quarter-finals.

When the domestic season ended, every English fan got behind the national team in the World Cup finals in France. David's involvement in the qualifiers had continued with some fine performances, particularly in the hard-fought 0-0 draw with Italy in Rome in October '97. That result sealed England's place at the top of the Qualifying Group Two contest.

By now, David appeared to be a permanent fixture in the England starting line-up. But in the build up to the finals, there were rumours that coach Glenn

Hoddle was thinking about dropping him for the opening game against Tunisia. The rumours were confirmed when David was replaced by Darren Anderton and watched the action from the bench – England won 2-0 with goals from Shearer and Scholes.

Along with almost everyone else, David puzzled over Hoddle's decision and two days later he vented his feelings at a press conference: 'I played in every game leading up to the World Cup finals,' he said. 'To be told that I was not in the starting eleven was pretty hard for me...I've had a few days to think about what I could have done wrong and I don't really know. The manager had a chat with me, but at the time I was still a bit gutted. He did not really give me a reason.'

David and Glenn later had a heart-to-heart chat and the coach assured the player that he would get his chance in France.

Next up, Romania in

MANCHESTER UNITED SEASON 1997-98

PREMIERSHIP   Position: 2nd

Date	Opponent			Score
10 Aug	Tottenham Hotspur	A	W	2-0
13 Aug	Southampton	H	W	1-0
23 Aug	Leicester City	A	D	0-0
27 Aug	Everton	A	W	2-0
30 Aug	Coventry City	H	W	3-0
13 Sep	West Ham United	H	W	2-1
20 Sep	Bolton Wanderers	A	D	0-0
24 Sep	Chelsea	H	D	2-2
27 Sep	Leeds United	A	L	0-1
04 Oct	Crystal Palace	H	W	2-0
18 Oct	Derby County	A	D	2-2
25 Oct	Barnsley	H	W	7-0
01 Nov	Sheffield Wed	H	W	6-1
09 Nov	Arsenal	A	L	2-3
22 Nov	Wimbledon	A	W	5-2
30 Nov	Blackburn Rovers	H	W	4-0
06 Dec	Liverpool	A	W	3-1
15 Dec	Aston Villa	H	W	1-0
21 Dec	Newcastle United	A	W	1-0
26 Dec	Everton	H	W	2-0
28 Dec	Coventry City	A	L	2-3
10 Jan	Tottenham Hotspur	H	W	2-0
19 Jan	Southampton	A	L	0-1
31 Jan	Leicester City	H	L	0-1
07 Feb	Bolton Wanderers	H	D	1-1
18 Feb	Aston Villa	A	W	2-0
21 Feb	Derby County	H	W	2-0
28 Feb	Chelsea	A	W	1-0
07 Mar	Sheffield Wed	A	L	0-2
11 Mar	West Ham United	A	D	1-1
14 Mar	Arsenal	H	L	0-1
28 Mar	Wimbledon	H	W	2-0
06 Apr	Blackburn Rovers	A	W	3-1
10 Apr	Liverpool	H	D	1-1
18 Apr	Newcastle United	H	D	1-1
27 Apr	Crystal Palace	A	W	3-0
04 May	Leeds United	H	W	3-0
10 May	Barnsley	A	W	2-0

FA CUP

Date	Opponent			Score
04 Jan	Chelsea	A	W	5-3
24 Jan	Walsall	H	W	5-1
15 Feb	Barnsley	H	D	1-1
25 Feb	Barnsley	A	L	2-3

COCA-COLA CUP

Date	Opponent			Score
14 Oct	Ipswich Town	A	L	0-2

Toulouse. David was still on the bench when the action started – then, on 33 minutes, Paul Ince sustained a painful ankle injury and Glenn Hoddle sent Beckham on in his place. Full of pent-up frustration and with a badly bruised ego, he had a lot to prove. His energy and determination added a certain zest to England's performance, and commentators were quick to point out that Hoddle's 'treat him mean, keep him keen' policy had done the trick!

The only disappointment was the result. After a close run contest with England in control, Romania snatched a 2-1 victory with Dan Petrescu's last minute strike.

Despite that setback England required just a single point from their last Group game, against Colombia in Lens and David started a match for the first time in the tournament. On 20 minutes, Owen crossed and Anderton smashed the ball into Colombia's net.

Ten minutes later Ince was fouled 30 yards out. Becks' free kick sailed over the Colombian wall, dipping into the top right hand corner of the net. It was a magnificent dead ball kick and it gave England the upper-hand. Hoddle's heroes protected their lead for the remainder of the match and Colombia hardly had another look-in.

Next, a Second Round meeting with Argentina at St Etienne where David patrolled the central midfield. On four minutes Danish referee Kim Nielsen awarded a penalty to Argentina when Seaman tripped Simeone. Batistuta thumped the ball home from the spot. Six minutes later Shearer did likewise for England after Owen had been tripped by Ayala.

In the 18th minute of this nail-biting encounter David chipped an inch perfect pass to Owen who beat two defenders than struck the finest goal of the tournament to give England a 2-1 lead. Argentina won a free kick just outside England's penalty area just before half time. Veron slid the ball to Zanetti who fired past a surprised Seaman to make it two-all at the interval.

A place in the quarter-finals was up for grabs.

CHAMPIONS LEAGUE

GROUP B - Position 1st

Date	Opponent			Score
17 Sep	Kosice	A	W	3-0
01 Oct	Juventus	H	W	3-2
22 Oct	Feyenoord	H	W	2-1
05 Nov	Feyenoord	A	W	3-1
27 Nov	Kosice	H	W	3-0
10 Dec	Juventus	A	L	0-1

QUARTER-FINAL

Date	Opponent			Score
04 Mar	Monaco	A	D	0-0
18 Mar	Monaco	H	D	1-1

The worst moment of David Beckham's career.

But, two minutes after the restart, things went horribly wrong for England and for David Beckham in particular. When he was bundled over by Simeone, referee Nielsen blew for an England foul. Then, in what can only be described as a rush of blood as he lay face down on the turf, David flicked up his right leg, making contact with Simeone, who behaved as though poleaxed. Nielsen reached into his pocket, flashed yellow at Simeone – and red at Beckham! The low point of David's career had arrived in his biggest game to date.

The game continued and went through extra time and into a penalty shoot-out. From the tunnel, David watched kick-by-agonising-kick – and when David Batty's effort was saved, England were on their way home two weeks earlier than planned. The contrite Beckham knew that he would definitely have taken his turn in the shoot-out – and the outcome might have been oh so different

Now all attention was focused on David's 'Moment of Madness'. If only he had kept his head, screamed the press. England, not Argentina, could be preparing to face Holland in the quarter-finals. He carried the can for the defeat. 'I'll always regret my actions,' he said. 'I have apologised to the England players and management, and I want every England supporter to know how deeply sorry I am.'

His parents tried to console him by telephone and even a trans-Atlantic conversation with his fiancée, Spice Girl Victoria Adams, couldn't dispel his despair.

Glenn Hoddle asked the fans to be sensible and understanding. 'It would be wrong to put the blame on his shoulders,' said the England boss while stressing that Beckham would be vitally important to England's chances in the next European Championship qualifying campaign.

FANTASY
FOOTBALL

Who would be in your dream team? Write the names of your chosen players on the shirts.

TIP: Be sure to use pencil so you can swap players around if you want to.

Use this blank strip to design your fantasy team kit.

TIP: Trace this page to make as many kits as you like.

A SUBLIM

SEASON

Winning back the Premiership title was great, but to win three trophies in 1998-99 was brilliant for Becks.

After the dramas of the World Cup finals in France, David faced an angry reaction back home. Many fans still felt that his sending-off against Argentina had ruined England's chance of glory.

To begin with he was barracked whenever he played in an away fixture and for a while it was touch-and-go whether he would move abroad and join one of the continental glamour clubs. In the end he decided to stay with United and face the music.

It was the right decision. Manchester United were about to enjoy their most successful season – ever.

Gradually, the World Cup furore faded and David missed just four of United's Premier League games during the 1998-99 season. His reading of the game and his passing were as sharp as ever and there were more spectacular goals adding to his tally. The first was a last-minute free kicked equaliser in the opening game against Leicester, for a share of the points in a 2-2 draw. Next came a 30 yard rocket in a 5-1 home win against Wimbledon in October. He didn't score again in the Premiership until the visit of Everton to Old Trafford in March, another of his trademark free kick specials – this one from 25 yards.

In the Premier League match at Selhurst Park against Wimbledon two weeks later, Becks scored United's goal in a 1-1 draw, with an outstanding performance from his old sparring partner Neil Sullivan, keeping the Dons the points.

There would be two more Beckham goals in the Championship race, a winner, from yet another free kick against Aston Villa at Old Trafford and the opening goal in the last match of the campaign against Spurs at Old Trafford. United had to win at all costs if they were to take the title. If they drew with Tottenham and Arsenal won their last game at Aston Villa then the Gunners would finish top. Talk about neck-and-neck!

Spurs scored first, through Les Ferdinand in 23 minutes. Then, three minutes before the interval, David hammered home past Ian Walker for a vital equaliser. United turned up the pressure after the break and just two minutes had passed when Andy Cole lobbed home the winner. United were champions for the twelfth time.

Three days later they had the opportunity to secure a second 'double' when they took on Newcastle in the FA Cup final at Wembley. David had not played in United's Third Round tie against Middlesbrough at Old Trafford when goals from Andy Cole, Dennis Irwin and Ryan Giggs took United forward – but he was fully involved in the rest of the Cup run. Liverpool were United's opponents at Old Trafford in Round Four and Michael Owen put them ahead after only three minutes. The scoreline stayed that way until, with just two minutes remaining, David launched a free kick that resulted in Dwight Yorke's equaliser. As the full time whistle approached super sub Ole Solskjaer netted a last-ditch winner.

Fulham waited in the Fifth Round. And Cole was the hero of the hour, scoring the only goal for United and setting up yet another journey to south-west London to face Chelsea in quarter-final. The Stamford Bridge tie ended in a 0-0 stalemate, and United won the replay 2-0 with both goals coming from Cole's strike partner Dwight Yorke.

It took United into the semi-final against Arsenal – United's third London-based opposition in the tournament. The match was played at Villa Park once again no goals were produced and the replay took place at the same venue three days later. This time David latched on to a great pass

from Sheringham and blasted the opening goal from 25 yards in the 17th minute. Arsenal pulled level through Dennis Bergkamp in the second half and the game went into extra time.

Now it was Ryan Giggs' turn to supply the magic with one of the best FA Cup goals ever seen. He ran almost 70 yards with the ball at his feet before evading two defenders and blasting the winner past David Seaman – a truly wonderful goal and United's ticket to that Cup final date with Newcastle.

Beckham and his team-mates desperately wanted to 'do the double' once more. But United's dream took on a rather nightmarish tone on six minutes, when Roy Keane came off the worse for wear in a collision with Newcastle's Gary Speed. Ferguson sent on Sheringham in place of Keano. David moved from right midfield into the centre with Ole Solskjaer taking up David's former position on the right.

Within a minute Teddy had the ball in Newcastle's net after connecting with a fabulous through pass from Paul Scholes. Fergie's unexpected ploy proved a stroke of genius. The re-shaped formation knocked Newcastle out of their stride and the Red Devils gradually took control. Paul Scholes added a second goal on 53 minutes – after Sheringham had supplied a telling pass. The scoreline stayed at 2-0 and Manchester United had their third 'double' of the '90s.

Amazingly, a once undreamed of 'treble' was now on the cards. United were next off to Barcelona for a European Champions Cup final meeting with Bayern Munich, so there was little time for celebrating the FA Cup victory.

United had started the Champions' League campaign at the Second Qualifying Round stage. David had played in both legs against LKS Lodz which United won with a 2-0 aggregate that took them into the Group D contest with Barcelona, Bayern Munich and Brondby. He then played in five of the six Group games, two victories and four draws that took them forward as runners-up to Bayern.

Beckham scored in Group games against Barcelona, and Brondby, but his best performance of the season came in the quarter-final home leg against Italian giants Inter Milan. In the opposition line-up was none other than Diego Simeone who had confessed that

A once undreamed of 'treble' was now on the cards.

he had stirred things up during their infamous World Cup clash.

David responded in the best way possible, with a truly breathtaking and inspirational performance in United's 2-0 victory at Old Trafford. After the match Becks and his Argentinian nemesis shook hands and swapped shirts. Two weeks later David was in the side again, as United held Inter to a one-all scoreline in Milan to progress to the last-four.

He then played in both legs of the semi-final against Juventus. The first match, at Old Trafford, ended 1-1 – thanks to Ryan Giggs' memorable last-minute equaliser. In the second leg the Italians led 2-0 after 11 minutes. But United were on fire and David was involved in the build-up to both goals that followed, from Roy Keane and Dwight Yorke. Andy Cole netted another six minutes from time . Now one more victory would complete that 'treble'.

The European Cup final in Barcelona marked United's third meeting of the season with Bayern Munich, but this was the most important match of the year for both sides. The Germans scored first through Mario Basler in the sixth minute and, despite relentless pressure from United, 88 minutes of agonising action passed with Bayern clinging to that slender lead.

Then in time added on, United won a corner. David took it as usual and the Bayern defence couldn't clear it. The ball fell to Ryan Giggs whose shot was blocked. It rebounded to Teddy Sheringham who coolly side-footed the long-awaited equaliser. Now the game was surely heading for extra time.

As the seconds ticked away, United won another corner. Again Becks took it. This time the ball found Sheringham. He flicked on to Solskjaer who jabbed home the all-important winner.

That strike completed the most dramatic comeback in European soccer history – and United had their hands on Europe's top trophy for the first time since 1968, a wonderful companion for the two domestic trophies already secure at Old Trafford. For David, whose season had started in the doldrums, it was a moment of supreme personal triumph.

MANCHESTER UNITED
SEASON 1998-99

PREMIERSHIP   Position: 1st

Date	Opponent			Score
15 Aug	Leicester City	H	D	2-2
22 Aug	West Ham United	A	D	0-0
09 Sep	Charlton Athletic	H	W	4-1
12 Sep	Coventry City	H	W	2-0
20 Sep	Arsenal	A	L	0-3
24 Sep	Liverpool	H	W	2-0
03 Oct	Southampton	A	W	3-0
17 Oct	Wimbledon	H	W	5-1
24 Oct	Derby County	A	D	1-1
31 Oct	Everton	A	W	4-1
08 Nov	Newcastle United	H	D	0-0
14 Nov	Blackburn Rovers	H	W	3-2
21 Nov	Sheffield Wed	A	L	1-3
29 Nov	Leeds United	H	W	3-2
05 Dec	Aston Villa	A	D	1-1
12 Dec	Tottenham Hotspur	A	D	2-2
16 Dec	Chelsea	H	D	1-1
19 Dec	Middlesbrough	H	L	2-3
26 Dec	Nottingham Forest	H	W	3-0
29 Dec	Chelsea	A	D	0-0
10 Jan	West Ham United	H	W	4-1
16 Jan	Leicester City	A	W	6-2
31 Jan	Charlton Athletic	A	W	1-0
03 Feb	Derby County	H	W	1-0
06 Feb	Nottingham Forest	A	W	8-1
17 Feb	Arsenal	H	D	1-1
20 Feb	Coventry City	A	W	1-0
27 Feb	Southampton	H	W	2-1
13 Mar	Newcastle United	A	W	2-1
21 Mar	Everton	H	W	3-1
03 Apr	Wimbledon	A	D	1-1
17 Apr	Sheffield Wed	H	W	3-0
25 Apr	Leeds United	A	D	1-1
01 May	Aston Villa	H	W	2-1
05 May	Liverpool	A	D	2-2
09 May	Middlesbrough	A	W	1-0
12 May	Blackburn Rovers	A	D	0-0
16 May	Tottenham Hotspur	H	W	2-1

FA CUP   Winners

Date	Opponent			Score
03 Jan	Middlesbrough	H	W	3-1
24 Jan	Liverpool	H	W	2-1
14 Feb	Fulham	H	W	1-0
07 Mar	Chelsea	H	D	0-0
10 Mar	Chelsea	A	W	2-0
11 Apr	Arsenal	H	D	0-0
14 Apr	Arsenal	H	W	2-1
22 May	Newcastle United	N	W	2-0

WORTHINGTON CUP

Date	Opponent			Score
28 Oct	Bury	H	W	2-0
11 Nov	Nottingham Forest	H	W	2-1
02 Dec	Tottenham Hotspur	A	L	1-3

CHAMPIONS LEAGUE   Winners

PRELIMINARY ROUND

Date	Opponent			Score
12 Aug	LKS Lodz	H	W	2-0
26 Aug	LKS Lodz	A	D	0-0

GROUP D - Position 2nd

Date	Opponent			Score
16 Sep	Barcelona	H	D	3-3
30 Sep	Bayern Munich	A	D	2-2
10 Oct	Brondby	A	W	6-2
04 Nov	Brondby	H	W	5-0
25 Nov	Barcelona	A	D	3-3
09 Dec	Bayern Munich	H	D	1-1

QUARTER-FINAL

Date	Opponent			Score
03 Mar	Inter Milan	H	W	2-0
17 Mar	Inter Milan	A	D	1-1

SEMI-FINAL

Date	Opponent			Score
07 Apr	Juventus	H	D	1-1
21 Apr	Juventus	A	W	3-2

FINAL

Date	Opponent			Score
26 May	Bayern Munich	N	W	2-1

BECKHAM FAMILY ALBUM

Hardly a day goes by without a new story about football's most famous couple. The world is fascinated by the lifestyle of David and Victoria...

Two happy events occured in the lives of David and Victoria in 1999. First, the birth of their bouncing baby boy, Brooklyn, on 4 March 1999.

Later that year – on 4 July – came their fabulous wedding in the romantic setting of an ancient Irish castle. This was a truly sumptuous affair – Victoria wore a £60,000 wedding dress, while David looked the part in an ivory suit that matched the bride's dress to perfection. Best Man Gary Neville delivered his speech wearing a Beckham-inspired sarong and the elaborate ceremony and reception was studded with stars from the worlds of sport and show-biz. The Wedding of the Decade meant that 'Posh and Becks' were now officially Mr & Mrs Beckham..

The happy couple and baby Brooklyn settled to a life of domestic bliss – despite the fact that life at 'Beckingham Palace', in Hertfordshire, became a constant source of fascination for press and public alike.

This splendid house – situated within easy reach of David and Victoria's two familes – has seven bedrooms, a snooker room, a tennis court, a gymnasium and a recording studio where Victoria creates her music.

There's also garage space for the Beckhams' fleet of cars which has included a Porsche 911, an Aston Martin Turbo, a Jaguar XXR a BMW XS, a Range Rover 4.6HSE – and a bullet-proof Mercedes.

The famous couple also have an luxurious apartment in Cheshire, within easy reach of Old Trafford.

David and Victoria are obviously happy with family life and they were thrilled with the arrival of their second son on 2 September 2002. They named him Romeo. "It's just a name we love," David explained. "It's always nervous having children, but it's the most beautiful thing in the world."

The Beckhams are now so famous that they have become a British institution. Now they're set to continue their reign in Spain.

It's as though they've always been around.

ANOTHER
TITLE

Winning the Premiership was becoming a happy habit for Becks' and his team-mates. They did it again, in 1999-2000.

As United's Premiership campaign unfolded in 1999-2000 David was again prominent, keeping up his usual high standards in 31 league appearances. He scored six league goals too, all in the second half of the season. The first was an 87th minute winner against Middlesbrough at Old Trafford in late-January. The 1-0 result restored United's place at the top of the Premier League table. When Becks scored again eight games later – the opener in a 2-0 victory at Leicester – they were still leading the pack while holding off strong challenges from Arsenal and Leeds.

Manchester United were unstoppable – their last nine league games of the season produced 32 goals. David chipped-in with four of them – in a 4-0 win at Bradford, a 7-1 thrashing of West Ham at Old Trafford, a 3-0 win in Southampton and a 3-1 home win against Spurs in the penultimate game of the campaign. It was the result against Southampton on 22 April that clinched United's sixth Premiership title in eight seasons, and they did it with four games to spare. David and his team-mates

collected their medals and the Premiership trophy after the meeting with Spurs on 6 May.

This was the season in which United did not compete for the FA Cup. Strangely, they were excused participation in the world's most famous domestic cup tournament so they could compete in the FIFA Club World Championship against South America's Copa Libertadores holders, Palmeiras of Brazil. David played in the big showdown in Tokyo in November '99, when a Roy Keane goal gave United a 1-0 victory and earned them the 'World Club Champions' accolade, the first British club ever to hold that title.

Becks was also involved in 13 of United's 14 games played in defence of the European Cup. They reached the quarter-finals where they met Real Madrid, holding them to a 0-0 scoreline in Spain, but losing their grip on the trophy in a 3-2 defeat at Old Trafford. A most disappointing exit from the competition.

Kevin Keegan, Glenn Hoddle's successor in the England manager's hot-seat, kept faith with Becks as England made it to

1.

second place in the Qualifying Group Five table. That took them into a play-off with Group Nine runners-up, Scotland.

The first game at Hampden Park on 13 November 1999 marked the first meeting of the old enemies since the Euro 96 finals when England had won en route to the semi-finals. This time England notched a 2-0 scoreline, both goals coming from David's United club mate Paul Scholes. In the second leg at Wembley, Scotland played their hearts out to secure a 1-0 victory, but it wasn't enough to halt England's progress to the Euro 2000 finals, jointly hosted by Belgium and Holland.

Unfortunately, Kevin Keegan and his squad endured a lean time in the Low Countries, losing to both Romania and Portugal in the Group A contest. The only bright spot of the summer for David and his team-mates was a 1-0 defeat of Germany in Charleroi, secured with an Alan Shearer goal that marked England's first tournament victory against the Germans since a certain game in 1966.

David had also played during the season against Argentina, Brazil, the Ukraine and Malta. He was now becoming a Three Lions regular. But, even the rising star Beckham could not have foreseen the next great honour that would come his way on football's international scene.

2.

Kevin Keegan, Glenn Hoddle's successor in the England manager's hot-seat, kept faith with Becks as England made it to second place in the Qualifying Group Five table.

1. Beckham on another surging run.

2. Celebrating yet another goal.

MANCHESTER UNITED
SEASON 1999-2000

PREMIERSHIP		Position: 1st		
08 Aug	Everton	A	D	1-1
11 Aug	Sheffield Wed	H	W	4-0
14 Aug	Leeds United	H	W	2-0
22 Aug	Arsenal	A	W	2-1
25 Aug	Coventry City	A	W	2-1
30 Aug	Newcastle United	H	W	5-1
11 Sep	Liverpool	A	W	3-2
18 Sep	Wimbledon	H	D	1-1
25 Sep	Southampton	H	D	3-3
03 Oct	Chelsea	A	L	0-5
16 Oct	Watford	H	W	4-1
23 Oct	Tottenham Hotspur	A	L	1-3
30 Oct	Aston Villa	H	W	3-0
06 Nov	Leicester City	H	W	2-0
20 Nov	Derby County	A	W	2-1
04 Dec	Everton	H	W	5-1
18 Dec	West Ham United	A	W	4-2
26 Dec	Bradford City	H	W	4-0
28 Dec	Sunderland	A	D	2-2
24 Jan	Arsenal	H	D	1-1
29 Jan	Middlesbrough	H	W	1-0
02 Feb	Sheffield Wed	A	W	1-0
05 Feb	Coventry City	H	W	3-2
12 Feb	Newcastle United	A	L	0-3
20 Feb	Leeds United	A	W	1-0
26 Feb	Wimbledon	A	D	2-2
04 Mar	Liverpool	H	D	1-1
11 Mar	Derby County	H	W	3-1
18 Mar	Leicester City	A	W	2-0
25 Mar	Bradford City	A	W	4-0
01 Apr	West Ham United	H	W	7-1
10 Apr	Middlesbrough	A	W	4-3
15 Apr	Sunderland	H	W	4-0
22 Apr	Southampton	A	W	3-1
24 Apr	Chelsea	H	W	3-2
29 Apr	Watford	A	W	3-2
06 May	Tottenham Hotspur	H	W	3-1
14 May	Aston Villa	A	W	1-0

FIFA CUP WORLD CHAMPIONSHIP
GROUP B - Position 3rd

06 Jan	Necaxa	N	D	1-1
08 Jan	Vasco da Gama	N	L	1-3
11 Jan	South Melbourne	N	W	2-0

WORTHINGTON CUP
13 Oct	Aston Villa	A	L	0-3

EUROPEAN SUPER CUP
27 Aug	Lazio	N	L	0-1

TOYOTA CUP
30 Nov	Palmeiras	N	W	1-0

CHAMPIONS LEAGUE
GROUP D - Stage 1 - Position 1st

14 Sep	Croatia Zagreb	H	D	0-0
22 Sep	Sturm Graz	A	W	3-0
29 Sep	Marseilles	H	W	2-1
19 Oct	Marseilles	A	L	0-1
27 Oct	Croatia Zagreb	A	W	2-1
02 Nov	Sturm Graz	H	W	2-1

GROUP B - Stage 2 - Position 1st

23 Nov	Fiorentina	A	L	0-2
08 Dec	Valencia	H	W	3-0
01 Mar	Bordeaux	H	W	2-0
07 Mar	Bordeaux	A	W	2-1
15 Mar	Fiorentina	H	W	3-1
21 Mar	Valencia	A	D	0-0

QUARTER-FINAL

04 Apr	Real Madrid	A	D	0-0
19 Apr	Real Madrid	H	L	2-3

THREE IN A ROW

2000-01 brought a third successive Premiership trophy for Man United.

The visit of Germany for England's first World Cup qualifier in October 2000 was to mark 'old' Wembley's last ever match. England were supposed to send the famous stadium off in a blaze of glory. Unfortunately the action on the pitch didn't follow the script – David and his team-mates suffered a 1-0 defeat, the goal coming in the 14th minute from Germany's Didi Hamman. To make matters worse manager Kevin Keegan shocked the football world by handing in his resignation within minutes of the final whistle.

Howard Wilkinson was given charge of the England team for the next World Cup qualifier, against Finland a few days later, and he saw them through a 0-0 draw in Helsinki. David didn't play, but he was back in contention for England's next game, a friendly against Italy in Turin.

The 15th of November 2000 turned out to be a significant date in the life of David Beckham – that was the day he was made England's captain by new caretaker manager Peter Taylor. Although surprised by the accolade and the trust placed in him by the temporary boss, David was in no way overawed by the responsibility that went with wearing the armband.

He took to the job with ease and exerted a calm authority over the predominantly young England side under his charge. At one point he even pulled back from a potentially volatile incident with a confrontational opponent. England may have lost 1-0 to Gattuso's goal, but the result didn't reflect on David – he would retain the armband each time he played in England colours.

Sven Göran Eriksson became England's latest coach in February 2001. Captain David and the boys welcomed him in the best possible way – with a 3-0 victory in a friendly against Spain at Villa Park. Becks was skipper in the first half of the season's other friendly, against Mexico at Derby's Pride Park, and he netted the third goal in England's 4-0 win.

But it was the World Cup qualifiers that really mattered. The next one was the return match against Finland at Anfield. Now England got back on course with a 2-1 win, although it all took too promising when Gary Neville put through his own goal after 26 minutes. But England rallied – Michael Owen equalised shortly before the break, and it was David, playing a true captain's role, who netted the winner on 50 minutes. Four days later things got even better with a win in Albania with goals from Owen, Scholes and Andy Cole.

Next Beckham scored the second goal on England's trip to Athens for a 2-0 victory against Greece. Waiting ahead in 2001-02 were crunch matches with Germany in Munich and with Greece at Old Trafford – two

by a 3-0 defeat of Sunderland at Old Trafford which took United to the top of the table – a position they would vacate just once during the remainder of the season.

United's seventh Premier League success in nine seasons and their third in a row, was made *almost* safe after a 4-2 win against Coventry at Old Trafford, in which David was a substitute. Confirmation came later that day when closest rivals Arsenal lost at Middlesbrough. The Premiership trophy was presented at United's next game, the local derby clash with Manchester City. This time around United had hit the pinnacle with *five* games still to play.

For David it meant a remarkable fifth Premier League champions medal in just eight

Bradford City were next – and they suffered a 6-0 defeat!

games that would heighten David Beckham's reputation even further.

Meanwhile, there was Manchester United business to attend to. After playing in the side that lost 2-0 to Chelsea in the FA Charity Shield match at Wembley in August, David had lined-up against Newcastle in the opening Premier League encounter of the new season, when he and his team-mates turned on the style to produce a 2-0 victory with goals from Ronny Johnsen and Andy Cole.

Newly promoted Ipswich were introduced to the sheer class of the reigning champions as David's stunning 30-yard free kick earned a draw at Portman Road. He netted in the next match too, against West Ham at Upton Park, although the Hammers fought back for a share of the points with two late goals.

Bradford City were next up – and they suffered a crushing 6-0 defeat in which David scored the sixth goal. That was followed

and a half years.

In the other domestic competitions the Red Devils were eliminated in the Fourth Round of the Worthington Cup by Sunderland, and by West Ham at the same stage in the FA Cup. United's European Champions' League adventure came to an abrupt and disappointing end just a few days after their league title celebrations. A 2-1 defeat at Bayern Munich in the quarter-finals sealed an aggregate victory for the German side that went on to win the trophy. En route to the last eight United had squeezed through the first Group stage, two points behind Anderlecht and one ahead of PSV Eindhoven.

In the second phase two victories against Sturm Graz and one against Panathiniakos, plus two draws with Valencia and one with Panathiniakos, were enough to take them into the last-eight against Bayern. But United's Euro dreams were now on hold, until the next time.

MANCHESTER UNITED
SEASON 2000-01

PREMIERSHIP   Position: 1st

Date	Opponent			
20 Aug	Newcastle United	H	W	2-0
22 Aug	Ipswich Town	A	D	1-1
26 Aug	West Ham United	A	D	2-2
05 Sep	Bradford City	H	W	6-0
09 Sep	Sunderland	H	W	3-0
16 Sep	Everton	A	W	3-1
23 Sep	Chelsea	H	D	3-3
01 Oct	Arsenal	A	L	0-1
14 Oct	Leicester City	A	W	3-0
21 Oct	Leeds United	H	W	3-0
28 Oct	Southampton	H	W	5-0
04 Nov	Coventry City	A	W	2-1
11 Nov	Middlesbrough	H	W	2-1
18 Nov	Manchester City	A	W	1-0
25 Nov	Derby County	A	W	3-0
02 Dec	Tottenham Hotspur	H	W	2-0
09 Dec	Charlton Athletic	A	D	3-3
17 Dec	Liverpool	H	L	0-1
23 Dec	Ipswich Town	H	W	2-0
26 Dec	Aston Villa	A	W	1-0
30 Dec	Newcastle United	A	D	1-1
01 Jan	West Ham United	H	W	3-1
13 Jan	Bradford City	A	W	3-0
20 Jan	Aston Villa	H	W	2-0
31 Jan	Sunderland	A	W	1-0
03 Feb	Everton	H	W	1-0
10 Feb	Chelsea	A	D	1-1
25 Feb	Arsenal	H	W	6-1
03 Mar	Leeds United	A	D	1-1
17 Mar	Leicester City	H	W	2-0
31 Mar	Liverpool	A	L	0-2
10 Apr	Charlton Athletic	H	W	2-1
14 Apr	Coventry City	H	W	4-2
21 Apr	Manchester City	H	D	1-1
28 Apr	Middlesbrough	A	W	2-0
05 May	Derby County	H	L	0-1
13 May	Southampton	A	L	1-2
19 May	Tottenham Hotspur	A	L	1-3

FA CUP

Date	Opponent			
07 Jan	Fulham	A	W	2-1
28 Jan	West Ham United	H	L	0-1

WORTHINGTON CUP

Date	Opponent			
31 Oct	Watford	A	W	3-0
28 Nov	Sunderland	A	L	1-2

CHAMPIONS LEAGUE

GROUP G - Stage 1 - Position 2nd

Date	Opponent			
13 Sep	Anderlecht	H	W	5-1
19 Sep	Dynamo Kiev	A	D	0-0
26 Sep	PSV Eindhoven	A	L	1-3
18 Oct	PSV Eindhoven	H	W	3-1
24 Oct	Anderlecht	A	L	1-2
08 Nov	Dynamo Kiev	H	W	1-0

GROUP A - Stage 2 - Position 2nd

Date	Opponent			
21 Nov	Panathinaikos	H	W	3-1
06 Dec	Sturm Graz	A	W	2-0
14 Feb	Valencia	A	D	0-0
20 Feb	Valencia	H	D	1-1
07 Mar	Panathinaikos	A	D	1-1
13 Mar	Sturm Graz	H	W	3-0

QUARTER-FINAL

Date	Opponent			
03 Apr	Bayern Munich	H	L	0-1
18 Apr	Bayern Munich	A	L	1-2

CAPTAIN OF THE LIONS

David was first awarded the captaincy of England by caretaker manager Peter Taylor ahead of the Friendly against Italy in Turin in November 2000. Watching from the grandstand was future England boss, Sven Göran Eriksson. The new supremo was so impressed with his display, that he kept David in the job each time he's worn a Three Lions shirt since then.

Now the England team just wouldn't be the same with out David performing the pre kick-off ritual – meeting the opposing skipper and the officials, exchanging pennants and calling heads or tail at the coin toss. He's also adept at those tricky after match interviews...

England Skippers

When he became the man-in-the-armband David joined an illustrious list of great players who have shared the honour. Here are the 41 England skippers since 1946...

George Hardwick (Middlesbrough)
Frank Swift (Manchester City)
Billy Wright (Wolves)
Alf Ramsey (Tottenham Hotspur)
Ronnie Clayton (Blackburn Rovers)
Johnny Haynes (Fulham)
Jimmy Armfield (Blackpool)
Bobby Moore (West Ham United)
Ron Flowers (Wolves)
Bobby Charlton (Manchester United)
Alan Mullery (Tottenham Hotspur)
Martin Peters (Tottenham Hotspur)
Colin Bell (Manchester City)
Emlyn Hughes (Liverpool)
Alan Ball (Arsenal)
Gerry Francis (Queens Park Rangers)
Kevin Keegan (Liverpool)
Mike Channon (Southampton)
Mick Mills (Ipswich Town)
Phil Thompson (Liverpool)
Trevor Cherry (Leeds United)
Dave Watson (Southampton)

Ray Clemence (Liverpool)
Peter Shilton (Stoke City, Southampton, Derby County)
Phil Neal (Liverpool)
Ray Wilkins (Manchester United, AC Milan)
Bryan Robson (Manchester United)
Terry Butcher (Rangers)
Peter Beardsley (Liverpool)
Gary Lineker (Tottenham Hotspur)
Mark Wright (Derby County)
Stuart Pearce (Nottingham Forest)
David Platt (Juventus, Arsenal)
Paul Ince (Manchester United)
Tony Adams (Arsenal)
Alan Shearer (Newcastle United)
David Seaman (Arsenal)
Sol Campbel (Arsenal)
Martin Keown (Arsenal)
DAVID BECKHAM (Manchester United)
Michael Owen (Liverpool)

ENGLAND

7

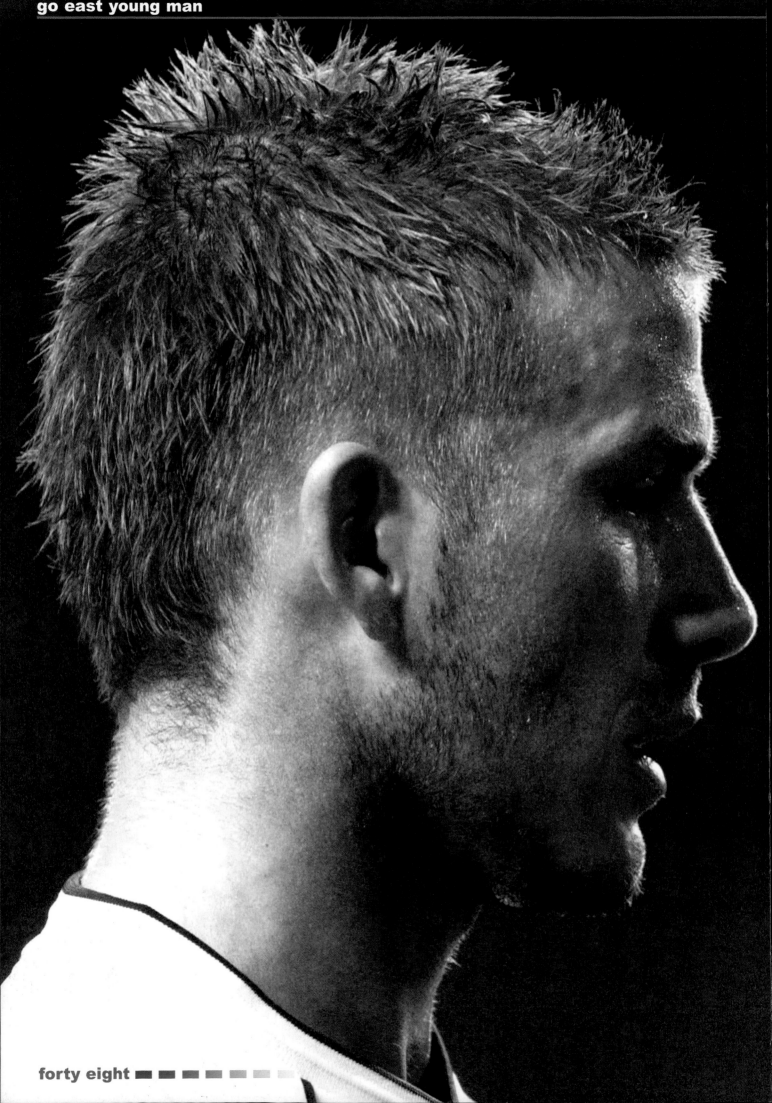

GO EAST YOUNG MAN

With the World Cup a year away, David and his team-mates would find 2001-02 particularly challenging.

David's 2001-02 season kicked-off with Manchester United's sixth consecutive appearance in the seasonal Charity Shield curtain raiser. And for the fourth time in a row they lost, this time by a 2-1 margin to FA Cup holders Liverpool.

A week later David lined-up against Fulham at Old Trafford, his 202nd League appearance for United. He scored his 43rd league goal, from one of those special free kicks of his – United's opening strike in a 3-2 victory. In the next game, at Blackburn, another Beckham free kick saved the day in a 2-2 draw.

In the first half of the season United fluctuated within the top six positions without actually hitting top spot. Things improved in the New Year when they were first for the first time after a 3-1 win at Southampton, in which David netted the second goal. They stayed in that familiar territory until a defeat at Middlesbrough in March dropped them down a notch, allowing Arsenal to overtake them and eventually take the title to Highbury, while United finished third. Arsene Wenger's superteam also won the FA Cup in which United were eliminated by Middlesbrough in the Fourth Round.

David's top performances of 2001-02 came in national colours as England sought to secure qualification for the 2002 World Cup finals in Korea and Japan in the remaining three Group 9 ties.

The first of these was arguably the toughest of the lot, the return match against Germany in Munich on 1 September 2001. In fact, it turned out to be one of English football's greatest nights – although it didn't look too promising when Germany scored first, through Jancker in the sixth minute. Six more minutes passed and Michael Owen redressed the balance in a move that started with a Beckham free kick.

A little later David fired only inches over the bar, then he supplied a cross to Emile Heskey and the burly striker almost connected. Deisler missed a sitter for the Germans and David Seaman pulled off a magnificent save just before the break. Then, with the half time whistle only a breath away, David sent in a cross to Rio Ferdinand who deftly nodded the ball to Stephen Gerrard on the edge of the area. From there the Liverpool man controlled and fired in a single swift movement and England were ahead.

Early in the second half David produced another precision pass, to Heskey who nodded down for Owen's volley to make it 3-1. In the 66th minute Owen collected another great pass, from his Anfield mate Gerrard, before completing his hat-trick. Eight more minutes passed with England dominant and the demoralised Germans wilting. Then, in the best move of the match, David and Paul Scholes exchanged passes before Scholes fed the ball to Heskey who completed a most unexpected rout by making it 5-1 to England. David gave another top notch performance in England's next Euro game, against Albania at St James' Park. England were in charge of the match, and Beckham took charge of England. He was involved in every promising movement, but the breakthrough was a long time coming. In the 44th Scholes' long pass found Owen who duly volleyed home the opening goal. England then endured a nervy second period in which Albania tightened their defence and twice went close. In the end Robbie Fowler wrapped it all up at 2-0 on 88 minutes.

The result and those all-important points meant that England and Germany were now neck-and-neck at the top of the group table, with England ahead thanks to a superior goal difference. Now it was all down to the last two games: Germany v Finland and England v Greece on 6 October 2001. Whoever came off best would be going to the finals, the other side would be condemned to battle it out in the play-offs.

David would not give up. He chased every ball and urged his team-mates ever onwards.

England met Greece at Old Trafford. Once again David put in a stunning Man-of-the-Match performance in a rather tricky encounter, in which the Greeks were on the top of their game and went ahead on 36 minutes.

With the score still at 0-1 after more than an hour of play, Sven sent on Teddy Sheringham, Moments later David picked him out with one of those famous free-kicks and the scores were level thanks to Teddy's clever header. But England's joy lasted about a minute – a failed clearance resulted in Greece regaining the lead. This was the worst possible news, especially as Germany were now level pegging with Finland.

David would not give up. He chased every ball and urged his team-mates ever onwards. It was poetic justice when, in the last minute, he lined-up for one last free kick with just over a minute to go. It was one of his best – ever – and it sailed into the Greek

goal for a two-all finish. Meanwhile Germany had also drawn in Finland which meant England were in the World Cup finals – thanks to David Beckham. Yet, for a while it was touch and go whether he would actually make it to the Far East. He had been fully involved in Manchester United's renewed challenge in the European Champions' League and their march to the quarter-final meeting with Deportivo La Coruna. After beating the Spanish side 2-0 in Spain, United lined-up for the return match at Old Trafford on 10 April 2002. In the 22nd minute David was tackled heavily by a Deportivo defender. He got to his feet and tried to carry on, but he was clearly unable to do so and the stretcher was brought on.

At first the United physio reckoned Becks would need at least eight weeks recovery time. Next day that estimate was reduced to six weeks. Over the coming weeks the progress of

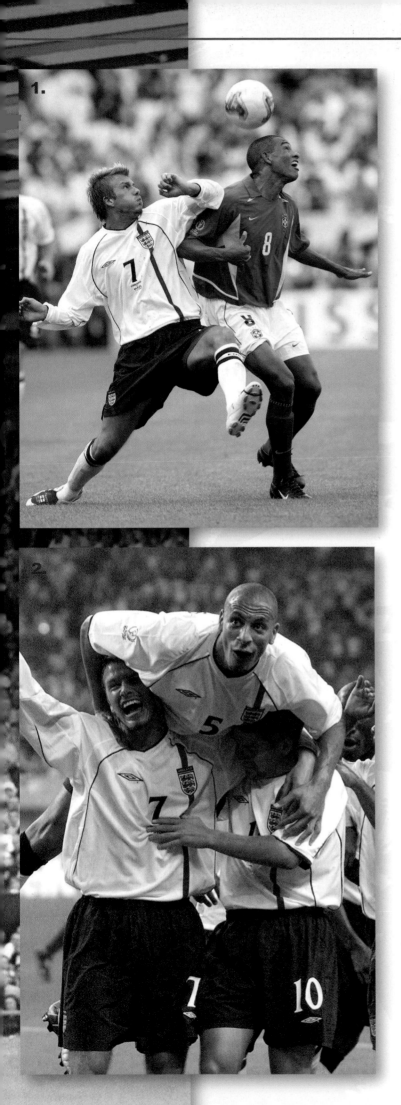

'Beckham's Metatarsal' made headline news in a running 'Will he, won't he?' story.

In the immediate aftermath of the injury David missed out on England's friendly with Paraguay at Anfield, but a more serious worry for Sven Göran Eriksson was that his star player and skipper might also miss out on the World Cup adventure in Korea and Japan.

In the event Beckham recovered in time to travel to the Far East, although he did not play in either of the pre-tournament friendlies against South Korea and Cameroon. But he was ready, able and willing when England's World Cup campaign began with the first Group F match against Sweden in Saitama.

England started full of fire and fight and on 24 minutes Sol Campbell headed home their first goal of the finals, from David's well-placed corner kick. After that England seemed to crumble with a bad case of the jitters and just before the hour Niclas Alexandersson capitalised on a defensive error to grab an equaliser. In the end it was left to David Seaman to save England's day – and the precious point.

Five days later David and the Boys did a lot better against mighty Argentina in the Sapporo Dome. England put in an amazing performance, one to equal the recent drubbing of Germany, producing a 1-0 victory – a slender scoreline that really didn't do justice to the overall effort by the team. The goal arrived shortly before half time. Pochettino tripped Owen just inside the penalty area and David lined-up to take the spot-kick. As he did so, Argentina's goalkeeper Cavallero and Beckham's old adversary Simeone, tried to put him off. But Beckham kept his cool and fired a bullet-like drive straight down the middle and into Cavallero's net.

Nigeria were next, in the last group game before the Second Round. The match was played in a stamina-sapping 34°C in Osaka. Michael Owen and Paul Scholes went close early on, with Nigeria's 'keeper Enyeama looking extremely nervous. Yet for all England's probing and prodding, the breakthrough never came, and the game ended scoreless, which meant a Second Round meeting with Denmark in Niigata.

Sven's men, were ahead within five minutes when a Beckham corner found Rio Ferdinand leaping to head goal-wards. Goalkeeper Thomas

1. Beckham in action against Brazil at the 2002 World Cup finals.

2. Celebrations after another England goal against Denmark.

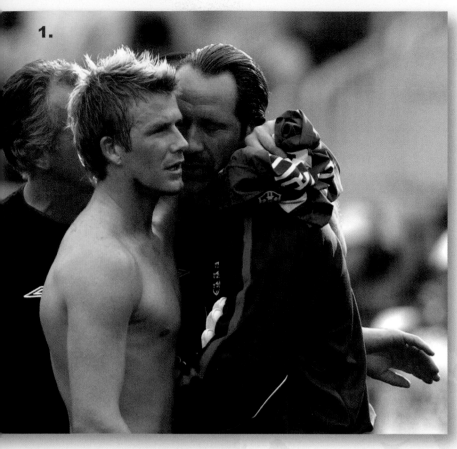

Sorensen failed to hold the ball and deflected it into his own net. A second goal arrived on 22 minutes when Trevor Sinclair found Nicky Butt in Denmark's danger zone. Butt flicked onto Owen who unleashed his shot into the bottom right corner of the Danish net. A further 22 minutes passed with England still in command, and just before half time Heskey collected a short pass from David just outside the area and made no mistake with a low hard drive past Sorensen for 3-0. England had beaten the Danish, but they still had to bring home the bacon – and that wouldn't be easy

1. Beckham consoles David Seaman after *that* freak goal by Ronaldinho.

2. Brazil celebrate World Cup victory against Germany. If only it had been England!

against quarter-final opponents Brazil in Shizuoka.

It all started so well. In the 23rd minute Michael Owen escaped his Brazilian marker Lucio to meet Emile Heskey's excellent through-ball and peel away to score past Marcos with a trademark strike. Then, in first-half injury time, Ronaldinho wriggled into English territory as defenders tracked back with him. Then he fed the ball out to his right where Rivaldo met it and delivered a left-foot shot past David Seaman to make it 1-1.

English hopes remained buoyant at the start of the second half. But disaster struck on 50 minutes. Brazil won a free kick some 22 yards from goal. As the players jostled for position Seaman stepped forward – presumably to check on his defensive 'wall'. Just then Ronaldinho quickly lobbed the ball over the defence and into the gap left between the stranded 'keeper and his goal and entered the top corner of the goal for 2-1.

That's the way the scoreline stayed and England's adventures in the Land of the Rising Sun were over. David and his Three Lions team-mates were saying 'Sayonara'. Brazil went on to beat Germany in the final and win the World Cup for a record fifth time; with two goals coming from boy wonder Ronaldo.

MANCHESTER UNITED SEASON 2001-02

PREMIERSHIP Position: 3rd

Date	Opponent			
Sun 19 Aug	Fulham	H	W	3-2
Wed 22 Aug	Blackburn Rovers	A	D	2-2
Sun 26 Aug	Aston Villa	A	D	1-1
Sat 08 Sep	Everton	H	W	4-1
Sat 15 Sep	Newcastle United	A	L	3-4
Sat 22 Sep	Ipswich Town	H	W	4-0
Sat 29 Sep	Tottenham Hotspur	A	W	5-3
Sat 13 Oct	Sunderland	A	W	3-1
Sat 20 Oct	Bolton Wanderers	H	L	1-2
Sat 27 Oct	Leeds United	H	D	1-1
Sun 04 Nov	Liverpool	A	L	1-3
Sat 17 Nov	Leicester City	H	W	2-0
Sun 25 Nov	Arsenal	A	L	1-3
Sat 01 Dec	Chelsea	H	L	0-3
Sat 08 Dec	West Ham United	H	L	0-1
Wed 12 Dec	Derby County	H	W	5-0
Sat 15 Dec	Middlesbrough	A	W	1-0
Sat 22 Dec	Southampton	H	W	6-1
Wed 26 Dec	Everton	A	W	2-0
Sun 30 Dec	Fulham	A	W	3-2
Wed 02 Jan	Newcastle United	H	W	3-1
Sun 13 Jan	Southampton	A	W	3-1
Sat 19 Jan	Blackburn Rovers	H	W	2-1
Tue 22 Jan	Liverpool	H	L	0-1
Tue 29 Jan	Bolton Wanderers	A	W	4-0
Sat 02 Feb	Sunderland	H	W	4-1
Sun 10 Feb	Charlton Athletic	A	W	2-0
Sat 23 Feb	Aston Villa	H	W	1-0
Sun 03 Mar	Derby County	A	D	2-2
Wed 06 Mar	Tottenham Hotspur	H	W	4-0
Sat 16 Mar	West Ham United	A	W	5-3
Sat 23 Mar	Middlesbrough	H	L	0-1
Sat 30 Mar	Leeds United	A	W	4-3
Sat 06 Apr	Leicester City	A	W	1-0
Sat 20 Apr	Chelsea	A	W	3-0
Sat 27 Apr	Ipswich Town	A	W	1-0
Wed 08 May	Arsenal	H	L	0-1
Sat 11 May	Charlton Athletic	H	D	0-0

FA CUP
Sun 06 Jan	Aston Villa	A	W	3-2
Sat 26 Jan	Middlesbrough	A	L	0-2

WORTHINGTON CUP
Mon 05 Nov	Arsenal	A	L	0-4

CHAMPIONS LEAGUE
GROUP G - Stage 1 - Position 2nd
18 Sep	Lille	H	W	1-0
25 Sep	Deportivo	A	L	1-2
10 Oct	Olympiakos	A	W	2-0
17 Oct	Deportivo	H	L	2-3
23 Oct	Olympiakos	H	W	3-0
31 Oct	Lille	A	D	1-1

GROUP A - Stage 2 - Position 1st
20 Nov	Bayern Munich	A	D	1-1
05 Dec	Boavista	H	W	3-0
20 Feb	Nantes	A	D	1-1
26 Feb	Nantes	H	W	5-1
13 Mar	Bayern Munich	H	D	0-0
19 Mar	Boavista	A	W	3-0

QUARTER-FINAL
02 Apr	Deportivo	A	W	2-0
10 Apr	Deportivo	H	W	3-2

SEMI-FINAL
24 Apr	Bayer Leverkusen	H	D	2-2
30 Apr	Bayer Leverkusen	A	D	1-1

THE REAL

After a thrilling and dramatic 2002/03 season, the Man United/Beckham love affair came to an end.

STORY

As the 2002-03 football season wound down to its fascinating conclusion, the fans of the world's best-supported soccer club suddenly found themselves with an extra worry on their minds. David Beckham, their most popular player, was going to leave Old Trafford...at least, that's what the newspapers were saying.

The nation's sports pages were full to the brim with tales of the multi-million pound transfer that would take the magical midfielder from Manchester United to Real Madrid. The reigning European champions were supposedly determined to capture the most prized signature in the modern game.

Nine months earlier, after England's World Cup adventures in Japan, all this speculation was a million miles away as David got back into action for United against Zalaegerszeg of Hungary, who produced a surprise 1-0 win in the first leg of the 2002-03 European Champions' League qualifying contest.

A few days later Beckham played his part as United's latest Premier League campaign got underway with a 1-0 win against newly-promoted West Brom at Old Trafford. But then, despite United's confirmation of a Champions' League place following a 5-0 2nd-leg thrashing of Zalaegerszeg – with David scoring again – things began to look a bit shaky for the club's Premier League ambitions.

A 2-2 draw at Chelsea with David netting one of the goals, was followed by a 1-1 scoreline at Sunderland. Things picked-up a bit when a Ruud van Nistelrooy secured a 1-0 home win against Middlesbrough and took Man United's points tally to a more respectable eight from four games. But two 1-0 defeats, at home against Bolton and away at Leeds, plunged the Old Trafford faithful into gloom and had the pundits proclaiming that United's glory days were over and done with.

David and his team-mates answered their critics with victories in their next five games, against Spurs, Charlton and Everton in the Premiership; Bayer Leverkusen and Olympiakos in the Champions' League. In the Everton match at Old Trafford, the scoreline was stuck at 0-0 with three minutes to go. Then United turned on the old magic and Paul Scholes scored three times before the referee's whistle finally put the Toffees out of their misery.

Another late-late show saved the points for United against Southampton in

early November. This time Diego Forlan netted an injury time winner. That triumph was followed by another setback, at neighbouring Manchester City. Kevin Keegan's Sky Blues stole the headlines with an impressive 3-1 scoreline. David wasn't in the team that day. but like everyone at United, he was shocked by the result. Sir Alex Ferguson later claimed that the local derby defeat was a turning point in United's season. 'We sorted a few things out in the dressing room,' he said.

Whatever was said behind those closed doors, it certainly did the trick as United were undefeated in their next ten matches and once again found themselves among the contenders in the Premiership and in Europe.

In the run-up to Christmas 2002, two defeats, by Middlesbrough and Birmingham, spelled the end of the good run and Arsenal emerged as favourites for the 2003 title. On New Year's Day, United were a goal down to struggling Sunderland with ten minutes to go and it looked as though the predictions were spot-on. It was then that David dug deep and produced a match-saving equaliser that was followed by an injury time winner from Paul Scholes. United were back on track and the pundits had to think again.

It wasn't such a buoyant story for David and his team-mates in the two domestic Cup competitions, although United did make it to the Worthington Cup final at the Millennium Stadium where they lost 2-0 to Liverpool. In the FA Cup, defeats of Portsmouth and West Ham took United into the Fifth Round where they faced holders Arsenal at Old Trafford – a fixture that would have particular reverberations for David.

Everyone knows that Alex Ferguson is not a good loser – it's one of the reasons that make him such a good winner. Like many a successful coach before

him, he often blows his top in the heat of those famous post-match dressing room 'discussions'. And that is reportedly what happened in the Old Trafford dressing room after Arsenal had knocked United out of the Cup. In his anger it seems that Fergie swiped a boot off a table. The flying footwear sailed through he air and struck the most prized player in British football just above his left eye, resulting in a nick that required medical attention.

The nation's press had a field day when David was photographed wearing a plaster over the cut. There were endless stories of a rift between the superstar footballer and the man who had guided him to the top. But as usual it all blew over and Fergie, David and the team knuckled-down to the rest of the season's work.

A string of good Champions' League results carried United through the two Group stages and into the quarter-finals in April – but there they were stopped by Real Madrid, the club at the centre of that 'Beckham's-on-the-Move' talk.

After the disappointment of Euro elimination it was back to the Premiership. Now it was a two-horse race between Arsenal and United who met at Highbury in a match dubbed the 'Face-Off'. In the end a 2-2 scoreline settled nothing and both clubs lived to fight another day.

It was still neck-and-neck on 26 April, when Arsenal travelled to the Reebok Stadium on to see a two-goal lead wiped out by a brilliant Bolton comeback. Meanwhile, Man United put themselves firmly in the driving seat by beating Spurs 2-0 at White Hart Lane. Now they just had to keep on winning and when David's 11th-minute goal went in against Charlton at Old Trafford, they were on the way, even though a goalkeeping error by Roy Carroll let in Claus Jensen for an equaliser two minutes later. United overcame that setback with a van Nistelrooy hat-trick sealing a 4-1 win.

CHAMPIONS LEAGUE

PRELIMINARY ROUND			Winners
14 Aug	Zalaegerszeg	A	W 0-1
27 Aug	Zalaegerszeg	H	W5-0

GROUP F - Stage 1 - Position 1st

18 Sep	Maccabi Haifa	H	W 5-2
24 Sep	Bayer Leverkusen	A	W 2-1
01 Oct	Olympiakos	H	W 4-0
23 Oct	Olympiakos	A	W 3-2
29 Oct	Maccabi Haifa	A	L 0-3
13 Nov	Bayer Leverkusen	H	W 2-0

GROUP D - Stage 2 - Position 1st

26 Nov	Basel	A	W 2-1
11 Dec	Deportivo La Coruna	H	W 2-0
19 Feb	Juventus	H	W 2-1
25 Feb	Juventus	A	W 3-0
12 Mar	Basel	H	D 1-1
18 Mar	Deportivo La Coruna	A	L 0-2

QUARTER-FINAL

08 Apr	Real Madrid	A	L 1-3
23 Apr	Real Madrid	H	W 4-3

Next day Arsenal handed the title to United with a 3-2 defeat by Leeds. On the last day of the season, against Everton, Becks was on top form as his superb free-kicked goal shortly before half time equalised Kevin Campbell's early strike for the Toffees. Later, van Nistelrooy notched his own 25th goal of the campaign to earn the new champions their 26th Premiership win of the season. After the match, David joined in the celebrations and then collected the sixth title medal of his career.

On the England front, he had worn the captain's armband in four of the five matches since the World Cup finals. He netted the opening goal of the Euro 2004 qualification campaign in a 2-1 victory in Slovakia. He was on target again in the next qualifier when Macedonia came to Southampton and bravely held the hosts to a 2-2 draw. It wasn't the best of starts for England, especially as Turkey were running away at the top of the table.

David played throughout the first half of the humiliating 3-1 friendly defeat by Australia at West Ham. It was an embarrassing result that acted as warning that was well and truly heeded.

David led the Three Lions to victory in Liechtenstein, where he was again on the scoresheet with a curling free kick in the 53rd minute of a 2-0 victory. Turkey's visit to Sunderland presented a different proposition, but the Beckham-inspired England produced their finest performance since beating Argentina at the World Cup 11 months earlier. It was a great game, but England left it late with substitute Darius Vassell pouncing on a loose ball to open the scoring on 75 minutes. Then, as the match wound towards its end, Kieron Dyer was brought down in the box. David stepped up and coolly converted the spot-kick for his fourth goal on the campaign. Now all that the Old Trafford faithful and every England fans could hope for was that their favourite son would stay in the country.

Now all that the Old Trafford faithful and every England fan could hope for was that their favourite son would stay in the country. But it wasn't to be. After almost two months of behind-the-scenes negotiations and press speculation, English football's Golden Boy was indeed off to ply his trade in Spain.

Nine times European champions Real Madrid finally captured the most coveted signature in the game in a £25 million transfer deal – meaning that our hero will line-up in the famous all-white strip alongside such world class stars as Ronaldo, Raul and Luis Figo. But he won't be wearing his familiar No.7 shirt – instead, David has been assigned number 23 in Real's squad of superstars.

David, Victoria and their boys will soon adapt to life in Spain's capital city and, if results go to plan, will soon be a hero of the Bernabeu. There's a Manchester United connection at the famous stadium, too. Soon after the Beckham signing, Sir Alex Ferguson's Old Trafford assistant Carlos Quieroz was named as Real's new coach.

There are exciting times ahead for David Beckham...

MANCHESTER UNITED
SEASON 2002-03

PREMIERSHIP   **Position: 1st**

Date	Opponent			
17 Aug	W.B.A	H	W	1-0
23 Aug	Chelsea	A	D	2-2
31 Aug	Sunderland	A	D	1-1
03 Sep	Middlesbrough	H	W	1-0
11 Sep	Bolton Wanderers	H	L	0-1
14 Sep	Leeds United	A	L	0-1
21 Sep	Tottenham Hotspur	H	W	1-0
28 Sep	Charlton Athletic	A	W	3-1
07 Oct	Everton	H	W	3-0
19 Oct	Fulham	A	D	1-1
26 Oct	Aston Villa	H	D	1-1
02 Nov	Southampton	H	W	2-1
09 Nov	Manchester City	A	L	1-3
17 Nov	West Ham United	A	D	1-1
23 Nov	Newcastle United	H	W	5-3
01 Dec	Liverpool	A	W	2-1
07 Dec	Arsenal	H	W	2-0
14 Dec	West Ham United	H	W	3-0
22 Dec	Blackburn Rovers	A	L	0-1
26 Dec	Middlesbrough	A	L	1-3
28 Dec	Birmingham City	H	W	2-0
01 Jan	Sunderland	H	W	2-1
11 Jan	W.B.A	A	W	3-1
18 Jan	Chelsea	H	W	2-1
01 Feb	Southampton	A	W	2-0
04 Feb	Birmingham City	A	W	1-0
09 Feb	Manchester City	H	D	1-1
22 Feb	Bolton Wanderers	A	D	1-1
05 Mar	Leeds United	H	W	2-1
15 Mar	Aston Villa	A	W	1-0
22 Mar	Fulham	H	W	3-0
05 Apr	Liverpool	H	W	4-0
12 Apr	Newcastle United	A	W	6-2
16 Apr	Arsenal	A	D	2-2
19 Apr	Blackburn Rovers	H	W	3-1
27 Apr	Tottenham Hotspur	A	W	2-0
03 May	Charlton Athletic	H	W	4-1
11 May	Everton	A	W	2-1

FA CUP

04 Jan	Portsmouth	H	W	4-1
26 Jan	West Ham United	H	W	6-0
15 Feb	Arsenal	H	L	0-2

WORTHINGTON CUP

05 Nov	Leicester City	H	W	2-0
03 Dec	Burnley	A	W	2-0
17 Dec	Chelsea	H	W	1-0
07 Jan	Blackburn Rovers	H	D	1-1
22 Jan	Blackburn Rovers	A	W	3-1
02 Mar	Liverpool	N	L	0-2

BECKHAM QUIZ

Test your knowledge of the world's most famous footballer with these 20 Beckham brainteasers...

1. With which team did David make his League debut?

2. Against which country did David make his first appearance as England's captain?

3. At which ground did young David once run out as Manchester United's mascot?

4. Which famous club hosted the European Cup final won by United in 1999?

5. Which England manager gave David his full international debut?

6. In which season did David collect his 'treble' medals?

7. At which French club ground was David sent-off during the 1998 World Cup finals?

8. Which England manager first appointed David captain of his country?

9. Which country did David and Victoria marry in?

10. Who did United beat in the 1999 FA Cup final?

11 Who were the opponents when David scored his 'wonder goal' in 1996-97?

12 Who was the goalkeeper against whom David scored his 1996 'wonder goal'?

13 What is David's starsign?

14 In which year did David first sign professional forms for Manchester United?

15 Against which Euro opponents did David score his first goal for United in 1994?

16 Who were the opponents when David made his England Under-21 debut in 1995?

17 Against which country did David make his full England debut in 1996?

18 Which team did United beat in the 1999 European Cup final?

19 Which London team did United beat to win the 1992 FA Youth Cup Final?

20 Who were England's last World Cup opponents?

SOLUTIONS

MATCH THE MATCH	TRUE OR FALSE?	SPOT THE DIFFERENCE	BECKHAM'S WORDSEARCH

MATCH THE MATCH
1. England
   v Greece
2. Man Utd
   v B Munich
3. Man Utd
   v Man City
4. England
   v Liechtenstein

TRUE OR FALSE?
1. False
2. False
3. True
4. True
5. False
6. False
7. False
8. True
9. True
10. True

SPOT THE DIFFERENCE

BECKHAM'S WORDSEARCH

QUIZ ANSWERS

1 Preston, 2 Italy, 3 Upton Park, the home of West Ham, 4 Barcelona, 5 Glenn Hoddle, 6 1998-99, 7 St Etienne, 8 Peter Taylor, 9 Ireland, 10 Newcastle, 11 Wimbledon, 12 Neil Sullivan, 13 Taurus, 14 1993, 15 Galatasaray, 16 Brazil Under-21, 17 Moldova, 18 Bayern Munich, 19 Crystal Palace, 20 Brazil